Praise for Donald S Murray's fiction

"A poignant exploration of love, loss and survivor's guilt." NICK RENNISON, *SUNDAY TIMES*

"Beauty, poetry and heart … a brilliant blend of fact and fiction, full of memorable images and singing lines of prose." SARAH WATERS

"A searing, poetic meditation on stoicism and loss." MARIELLA FROSTRUP, BBC RADIO 4

"A poignant novel." NICOLA STURGEON

"I loved this book." DOUGLAS STUART, AUTHOR OF *SHUGGIE BAIN*

"A classic bildungsroman … the kind of book … that can enrich your life." ALLAN MASSIE, *SCOTSMAN*, BEST BOOKS OF 2018

Praise for Donald S Murray's previous books
"Deeply moving." WILL SELF, *DAILY TELEGRAPH*

"The story is told with great charm, and tinged with a spirit of loss and yearning." PHILIP MARSDEN, *SPECTATOR*

The Man Who Talks to Birds

Donald S Murray

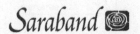

Published by Saraband,
Digital World Centre,
1 Lowry Plaza,
The Quays, Salford, M50 3UB
www.saraband.net

ISBN: 9781913393144

1 3 5 7 9 8 6 4 2

Printed and bound in Great Britain by
Clays Ltd, Elcograf S.p.A.

To my brother Peter,
who has a more genuine claim
to this title than I have

and to the staff of the English Department
in Anderson High School, Lerwick,
whom I worked alongside for
some of these months.

Foreword

The geography of islands has changed over the past year.

Drive down the roads that run their width or length and you might not be able to see this. The villages or crofthouses look much the same as ever. The moor possesses identical shades to those it possessed the year before – the purple blaze of heather in August, the muted green at the edge of lochs or the heart of bogland. The same is true of the fields stretching out within crofts. Sheep graze there as they have done for decades. Wild iris flowers beside streams.

And yet the sea surrounding the islands has imperceptibly widened. The distance between local and mainland airports has stretched a little, too. The signs and symptoms of this can be seen in the sharp reduction in the number of camper vans and tourist buses making their way along the highways and byways of a place like Shetland, either as a result of island ferries or flights. Fewer cars have made their way from the island's rural areas to the main town of Lerwick at the start and end of each working day.

History has become slower, too. The fact that there are fewer vehicles has made it seem as if our age has travelled in reverse over the past few months and we have somehow swapped places with our ancestors. We walk more, going down the village road, say, to the shoreline with greater frequency than we have done for decades. We talk more, leaning on croft or garden fences to speak to our neighbours, being drawn once more into the tight, confining world we thought we had left a generation or so ago. No longer having to go into town for work or even shopping, we have become more generous with the time we give one another, far less mean with either the words or attention we grant to those we meet upon our way.

At least, that was how it was for me and for many others I have encountered within the past year. In some ways, I have started to resemble my father. Walking down the road with my dog at my heels, I have found myself noting changes in the wind and weather in the way he did, spotting clouds growing thick and dense, waves starting to stir, noting the way, too, in which flocks of sheep or birds congregated in a field in anticipation of the arrival of a storm. As a result of this, I have conjured up poems in much the same way as he used to consider God and faith in the prayers that came to his mind some forty years ago, conscious that there is not as much difference between them as a layman might think. The two continually edge their way into each other's territory.

The following poems have been – in the main – inspired by walks through this village, passing the gardens of neighbours, the track that runs beside the shoreline, seeing the cluster of rocks on the water's edge, the rack and ruin of the old Parliamentary Church in one of its fields, the swoop of terns as I step near their nests.

At first, they were not intended for publication. Instead, they were simply short verses of contemplation shared with my friends. This changed as both poems and days in lockdown grew in number, those I knew informing me – both privately and publicly – how they appreciated work that was simultaneously a diary, a record of the natural world I witnessed on my journey and the thoughts these encounters inspired. I am grateful to all those who provided me with encouragement in creating them: my circle of friends here and elsewhere, especially my wife Maggie and my publisher Sara Hunt at Saraband. I am conscious that I have a very different life from those who have an urban existence. There are times – over the past few years – that my location has been a major disadvantage with ferries and flights adding hours and miles to some of my journeys.

This year, however, it has been a blessing. This year it has been an escape and relief.

Donald S Murray

Quarff,
Shetland

November 2020

April

Awakenings

At six o'clock (or so) this morning,
they broke out of social isolation,
their songs a mix of celebration,
wooing, warning
as they rejoiced in close proximity
within a garden edged by trees.

Did I envy them – these starlings, sparrows?
Yes – for the way they recklessly embraced
their neighbour's feathers,
squabbled beak to face,
swirled into the distance.

Unlike those of us who've bunkered down,
the grounded human race.

Quarff in Quarantine – 2020

And here we are, transported to our fathers' age,
confined to our eight acres, caged
within croftland, talking across a neighbour's
    fence in soft
rain or sunlight. Soon we'll cross

back into their time, speak of hours
employed on the hydro-dams, bringing power
to darkened peaks and glens, recall, too,
    Merchant Navy decks,
years in hotels or service, check

there's enough feed for every brood of hens
pecking around manure heaps, knowing we
    depend
on the shit-smeared eggs and plucked flesh
we harvest from these birds, no longer now
    emmeshed

by all that once pressed hard upon us.
A new birth and new beginning.
Different, terrifying, fresh.

Small Comforts in the Time of Coronavirus

Space contracts. Ferries rust in harbour,
held at bay
by governmental order,
while planes no longer venture near Sumburgh or
   Stornoway.
Soon it's said, there's plans
to disconnect all railway-lines
criss-crossing continent or mainland.
Within a few years time,

motorways will disappear.
(Already we see buses roll on empty,
while taxi-drivers rarely move from first gear
in the hope that they might see

the prospect of an occupant to fill an empty seat.)
And in that process time expands.
We slow our step, drag our feet
to journey across islands,

taking hours
to appreciate the wind and birdsong,
scent of flowers,
the wonders that our ancestors glimpsed

that we thought had gone.

May

One

This morning brings the return of winter's chill.
It makes tulips bend and buckle,
bows low hosts
of golden daffodils

in both our and neighbours' gardens.
Perhaps we should go and lockdown,
bolt in place every bud
and stalk we pass on our walk round

the village,
making sure storms wreak no further violence
against small signs of spring
glimpsed these last weeks

of which only a few flowers remain,
sheltering against wall and fence
as winter's storms curl round again.

Two

Today I saw myself as I might have been
some fifty years ago, a youngster clambering rocks
as he slipped the ties that bind
their kind these days round laptop screen and X-box.
Who knows what he'll find
as he explores both moor and shoreline,
ignoring the chill of the occasional snowflake
whirling like these terns reeling round the nearby beach?
I saw, too, a cock-sparrow among branches,
a clutch of buds and blossoms crammed within his beak,
scratching out a nest he'll build now and in the coming weeks,
like that young lad preparing for his future
scaling rock and wondering how much farther he can reach.

Three

a

For a long time, I thought the seals had been
   displaced
by returning terns, imagining these birds soaring
   up to chase
stout intruders from the rocks on which they
   often lie outstretched,
wings sweeping down to clear them from the
   crags they hoped to pitch

their nests. But I was wrong. Today the seals are
   back
to coast and wallow, ignoring too the dark
heads and cries of those that shriek and swirl,
claiming sole possession of this edge of their salt
   world.

b

Today the world's untroubled by the sound
of engines, chainsaws, lawnmowers powering
    over old ground,
cutting each blade neat and short.

Instead our ears are filled
with bird-calls: the bickering of gulls,
sweep of curlew, the curt

interruption of a crow; cheep of starlings,
    sparrows.
Around our home, we hear cries ebb and flow
within a quiet undisturbed

by all man has made for centuries.
No stirring or suggestion of a human deed or
    word.

Four

a

Today I noticed on my morning walk
how cobwebs can lace
together heather-stalks
on still days like these,

spiders imitating clouds
that clamp us down,
knitting funeral-shrouds
for insects scrambling round

the edges of moor,
mimicking that mist we sometimes feel
has trapped us in this village,
having strolled these same roads

a thousand times before.

b

A cuckoo's come to visit Quarff,
calling out incessantly, a mocking laugh
at humans unable now to follow their chief rule
and step near a neighbour's nest.

Its cry could try our patience,
a plague, a nuisance, curse,
till we realise its notes resemble
the rhythm of the human heart.

Five

Boulders pitched upon the edge of Quarff
visited on this grey morn
are stark reminders of an hour
when earth was split and torn
by fire and flame, the fragments of old rocks
patterning each monolith of stone.

A recollection, too, that despite the surface calm
we've stood on the periphery of havoc
for centuries. Crofters round here
spoke of storm and pestilence, the coming shock
of war. Small birds tried
to guard their nests among these rocks
from skuas, gulls and hooded crows.
Despite our long complacency, these boulders act
as admonitions, warning of what we've always –
    deep down – known.

Six

Today the terns disturbed our peace
feasting near the shoreline
in a continual swirl, the screech
of beaks accompanying flight as they plunged
    time

and time again into a shallow stretch of sea,
with wings stretched in benediction, giving
    thanks and prayer
for silver, the grace and charity
brought by tide and current, the blessings

that the ocean sometimes bears.

Seven

This morning gulls' cries led the call to fight
when a pair of strangers edged into the sight
of birds nesting on the shoreline. These dark
   invaders
hard to recognise. No slashes – I could see
   – emblazoned
on either side of wing. Their menace, though,
   more plainly seen
by those settled on the beach as they flew to
   isolate and quarantine
them, guarding chick and nest upon the ground
in that skirmish in the heavens, fierce artillery of
   sound.

Eight

Over the last few months, Charon
has dragged his galley through this portage
that some have told me is also known
as the 'valley of dry bones'.

I have not seen him. Not bow or keel
of the ferry he keeps corpses stacked within,
though I've been conscious
of his presence in the still

and storms of spring. And not just here
but everywhere for the waters of the Styx
and Acheron have spilled their banks
and given weight and substance to the tears

of those who have lost friends and kin
to plague and pestilence,
the final breath of those whose lives
have ended in isolation,

the wards and rooms they've been trapped in
while waiting for the coming of that vessel,
knowing their final voyage
will – very soon – begin.

Nine

Each lockdown day I've been in danger of
   becoming
that odd man who talks to birds,
listening to the sparrows' chit-chat,
circulating rumours overheard

from the beaks of terns; sympathising too
with oystercatchers chased and harassed
by others; the turnstone feigning injury
until it's sure intruders have walked past

its chicks; practising diplomatic skills among
squabbling starlings: granting counsel to the
   grief
and cries of curlews; suffering the delusion
of being one who can bring peace to both birds
   in flight and all that nests beneath.

June

One

Every morning I'm awakened
by a soundtrack of sparrows
echoing from the narrow
stretch of trees around my home.

This day is no different:
notes interspersed by larksong,
curlew-cries, just like every morning that's gone
past for the last few months, the pattern of
   existence known

(almost) in advance. Yet today seems different.
I interpret each sound, vivid, clear,
as some sort of commemoration for my years
upon the planet, a special birthday track

these birds have played just to remind me
that while time's still moving forward,
there is no chance it ever will move back.

Two

There are two ways of acquiring wisdom.
One – they say – is travelling far and wide.
The other is to stay in a location,
focusing ears and thought and eyes

on all that surrounds you in the one place
in which you choose (or are forced) to bide,
noting how the seasons slide
into each other,
the rise and fall of wind or cloud or tide,
taking account of changes
and allowing them to guide
the path on which you step and stride.

Someday, though my friends would all deny it
(indeed, it would be to their great surprise),
I'll have circled all the tracks around this
    township
and discover I am well and truly wise.

Three

When I was still in primary school,
those a decade older, not my peers,
used to practise a loud yodel,
sing Slim Whitman and Hank Williams songs
with one about a lonely whippoorwill
curling upwards in the sky.

Nowadays, when I set off on strolls,
the curlew and the snipe
accompany my footfall,
their notes so loud and clear
that I think of those ten (or more) years older,
some still familiar faces, others I've passed by,
self-isolating, shielded,

so lonesome they could cry.

Four

Behind our house, bog-cotton white
in the peat-dark ground
star and comet bright
shining when both rain and cloud
grind earth-locked spirits down.

And then a twist of road,
a slow swerve round a corner,
flakes of sun are found
within a field of buttercups
in a sodden stretch of ground
with glints of tormentil,
a rare monkey-flower,
the blackbird's yellow beak
pecking at the greyness of our mood
with its mellow range of sounds.

Five

Sometimes I feel I have become someone like my
    uncle
with binoculars upright upon a window sill,

allowing him to take note of all that might occur
upon the village road. He'd spot speeding cars

and wonder where they were going in such hurry,
see couples stepping off the bus, the shopping
    bags they carried

and contemplate the bargains that could be
    stuffed within.
With me, mostly, it's the birds that spin,

rise and dip around the shoreline, tankers
    anchored and still
not that far from our garden. They will wait there
    till

lockdown's ended, when oil prices – once again –
    might rise
when they will move from here like herring boats
    once did

shifting outwards on a long-awaited tide.

Six

This evening an encounter I did not expect,
an intruder with the lustre of an angel
sweeping down on Quarff – a great white egret
exiled on the shore here,
a wide-winged, sharp-beaked stranger
with the other birds reacting as humans
   sometimes do,
perceiving its arrival a constant threat and
   danger
to the future prospects of their young.

I watched gulls take on the guise of sentries,
terns blitz and throng
its flightpath,
the rock on which it stood,
trying to make sure
it would jet off quickly
to whichever part of heaven
it had first hailed from.

Seven

They once thought heaven's boundaries lay
just above the startling heights
where the lark sang to mark the start of day,
dancing within the trembling light,
signalling, too, the loosening clutch of night …

And I could well believe it,
for there is something in the flight
of birds that convinces humans we can receive
the gift of wings, that somehow, too, we might
aspire to crests and summits where within our
   sight,

the sparrow soars triumphant,
the starling, collared dove and gull
mimic the arc of angels,
the flexing of their quills,
allowing them to spread out
and stretch to span the world.

Eight

Each clump of heather
a clenched fist
punching its weight
out from peat.

Each knotted stem's
a twisted muscle
drawing strength
from the stored heat

of darkness,
the layers of centuries,
rot and decay,
loss and grief,

until in August,
it alters shade,
no longer strictly brown or green,
a mingling of leaves,

but with burnished red
and purple flowers,
as if some bloodshed in the past
from the earth has seeped.

Nine

There is something Pentecostal in the daylight of
   the north
with dawn granting a vocabulary that all can
   understand
with the solitary exception of man,
yet even we hear new voices that fill both air and
   earth,

though excluded from their company, barred
from dialogue with the sparrow, starling, lamb,
their songs of devotion, loud calls of alarm
as remote to us as moonlight, the far-off gleam
   of stars,

while flowers lose their customary quiet,
their leaves and petals drawing bees and birds
with promises, flames of colour with a gift of
   words
heard only by those who come to feast upon
   their light.

Yet mainly it is our feathered messengers that sing
circling round us with their panoply of sounds
that build new towers of Babel on this ground,
layering their creations with the thrust and
   flutter of their wings.

---

*Contrary to the suggestion in this poem, scientists believe that, with
the exception of alarm calls, birds do not understand the cries of any
other species than their own.*

Ten

Today everything's transformed: the fleece of
  sheep
mingling with cloud. Waves rippling on the beach
bearing a similar shade. When all is quiet and hush,
land and sea impossible to make out or
  distinguish.

Within that blur of greyness, the redshank struts.
We glimpse it on a fence-post – how that small
  head juts
back and forth as it takes time
to probe the world around it, both dark shade
  and tiny sign
of light until the damp gloom of the hour's
altered by its dance, the power
of thin legs kicking, a flash of scarlet stockings
  rising from the land
to give all who watch it impressions of the
  Moulin Rouge or ceilidh dance

with imitations of a jig or reel, the high jinks of
  the can-can.

Eleven

The cries of gulls
a peal of bells
as they ring loud in alarm
to warn
their neighbours of a bonxie's flight
as it swept inland that morn.

They guard nest and chick
with a stretch of wings
spreading outwards from the beach
to the roof and walls
of Quarff's old crumbling kirk;
each cry a strident pitch
for mercy,
a protest and a plea
for their kind's protection
whichever way that predator
might choose
to plunge and fall.

Twelve

Terns are alarmed by the proximity of sheep.
They swirl down upon them,
clipping horn and fleece with beaks
sharpened on a ledge of rock
for use upon these flocks
that seem to threaten nestlings when they graze,
clearly suffering nightmares of distant days
when giant Cheviot, Suffolk, Blackface
crunched upon egg-shells,
slipped egg-whites and yellow yolks
down wooly throats,
feasting on their offspring
like the buttercups and dandelions
ground by teeth
flowering every summer on this coast.

Thirteen

On the edge of vision, the wonderful occurs.
Whales skirt the jagged shoreline. Rare birds
skip and dance on land. But I seldom see them,
    coming face
to face instead with the familiar, the
    commonplace,
the miracles of orchids on the roadside, the
    puffballs
of dandelions, how parachutes of seeds rise and
    fall
on a breeze, how, too, the ringed plover feigns
injury as it races to mislead me through a smirr
    of mist and rain.

These moments matter more to me than any
    hurried contact
with the rare and strange. My daylight
    encounters with the lark
and hooded crow, sparrow and collared dove
among the instances that grace my life, among
    the times I love.

Quarff: Dandelions

These dandelions by the side of the road
each day show
what occurs to people
as their lives come and go.

First of all, the glow
and gold of youth; that slim, resilient stalk
encountered in the brisk walks
of our early days,

and then each flower's head turns grey,
and we can only watch and ponder
as storms puff
and blow their white and silver crowns away.

Outside Time

One

Water swirled around the island coast
these days that clouds hang thick, moist
coats about us. We thought the tide
was suffocating life on land, rising high
and locking every movement of our limbs
more strictly than the times we lived within,
compelled to swim each hour we tried to walk
past neighbours' homes, making bubbles when
  we talked
to one another, sweeping feet and hands
through the prevailing current, wondering if
  we'd ever once again
have the chance to stand on this unfamiliar land.

Two

These walks can lead me somewhere intangible
to spaces often frequented by gannet, tern or gull,
neither constant sea or land, where even sunlight
    can be dulled
and made vague and uncertain by the swirl and
    swathe of waves.

Familiar music comes to mind and takes hold.
Van Morrison who both challenges and consoles
listeners with the thought that we dwell here on a
    threshold
balanced between a mother's birth-pangs and the
    grave.

Life's insecure as any coastline. We're all too aware
    the pound
of waves can break through boulders, flood walled
    and cultivated ground,
seize pier and harbour, swallow steel hulls down.
And we are just as fragile – though we try each
    day to brave

life's dark distinctions, we are constantly aware the
    moment will arrive
when we can slip off that threshold, be swept by
    the tide,
occupy that unsafe spot where both gull and
    gannet dive.

Fashion in the Age of Coronavirus

The village women used to fasten knots
in coloured fabric tight around their throats
to keep their perms in place
through unsettling storms.

All different these days, for the purpose
of these scarves is to keep nose
and mouth confined in case foul air finds its way
into flesh and soul. Time has transformed

existence. Even of that simple square
of cloth for now female heads lie bare,
while both genders wear them like bandanas,
stepping into small town shops, braving

empty city streets – if both nerve and spirit dare.

Fashion in the Age of Coronavirus 2

Even air can give people the vapours
during these times, this troubled year

which is why we wear masks of cloth or paper
to keep airways crisp and clear

of the uncanny threat that plagues us
for all we're often unaware and blind

of how its presence looms to choke and gag us,
overwhelming heart and lung and mind.

His Life in Quarantine

A neighbour pined so much for visitors
that he sketched out faces on a kitchen wall
to conceal a stain there. He'd remain
for hours to talk to them until he called

upon the relatives he'd painted in his sitting
   room
to exchange the time of day. He heard
from them the latest news, and thought it all
   more satisfying
than the continual cries of birds

outside the window. No one thought to ask
what he'd drawn inside his bedroom, what kind
   of company
looked down on his sheets and blankets,
pillows propping up his elbows as he shared
   deep intimacies.

His Life in Quarantine 2

Brooding, bearded,
an old Guizer Jarl
feared
being trapped on this far rim of the world,

and so he took out his helmet,
winged and plumed,
to see if its presence might permit
his escape from rooms

where he'd been long confined.
He placed it on his crown,
allowing eyes and mind
to spin round

the places
where he'd seen of late
a black-backed gull giving chase,
greylag geese as flocks migrate.

Soon a miracle occurred.
These great wings
began flapping.
He took off like a bird

touring distant outposts,
allowing him to explore and invade
a thousand shorelines, coasts
ancestors might have gone near when they made

their long-forgotten Viking raids.

Three

Cabernet Franc. Merlot. Muscat blue.
Thick clusters on the moor.
This year's blooms of heather viewed
in richer shades than ever glimpsed before
upon this soil,

purple hues that compensate
those compelled to stay at home,
unable to vacate
their homes and exchange
the flurry of a summer storm,
the occasional whip of rain
for locations where both heat and warmth recur,
where sun reigns
time and time again.

And so the moorland seeks to imitate
those moments that householders missed
throughout these last few months at home;
these blossoms transformed
into crops fit for port or claret,
bubbles for a strange and dark champagne,
Shiraz or Cabernet Sauvignon,
which those who stay here sip and relish
time and time again.

Four

Throughout lockdown,
she welcomed round

departed friends and relatives
who arrived with gifts

of small talk
following a short walk

from the local graveyard.
They all agreed that life was hard

these days,
remaining in one place

with no prospect of escape
from the boundaries of the village,

until one corpse (long still) declared
'I never went anywhere

during my time above ground.
Not even a quick spin around

the borders of the island.'
And so he failed to understand

the whole sad substance of her complaint,
as all his days of life and death he'd suffered

a similar confinement and constraint.

Quarff – a reflection

This has been a year when it has once again
   been possible
to contemplate the prospect of careers
as hermits, solitaries or anchorites,
when experience has taught us to no longer fear
a future walled within a cell,
hidden way beyond the sight
of others with only prayer to light
and guide us, keep us guarded from all ill.

And that is why we might come yet to identify
with St Katherine of Ledbury, Kevin of
   Glendalough,
fingers stretched in worship or for small birds
   to fly
and touch down on our palms,
enticing them with dried fruit,
a scattering of grain,
the gentle rendition of a hymn or psalm

until the air is filled with voices
with a different tone and pitch
to the human speech with which
we were long accustomed
before these days of isolation,
these times when our lips have been stitched
tight with layers of cloth or paper

and we can only hear a medley of bird-calls,
the mewling gulls, the curlew's tears, the
    sparrow's constant chirp.

Oystercatcher

a

The oystercatcher probing through grey stone
    and sand
to find limpets or mussels it can eat,
prising open shells with the sharp edge of its
    beak
resembles us as we sift through the detail of the
    weekend news,
each grey grain
of grim discomfort, to find if bright remains
to feed and elevate us, keep wing and spirit
    high,
help us focus on the sunrise that shades this
    morning's sky.

b

Oystercatcher, lift our thoughts
as once you raised St Bridget and her boat
when dark waves threatened,
keeping her afloat,
for we have need of wings once more
to flutter round life, accompanying us to shores
that have been closed, confined of late
but can be opened up once more
by the pliers of your beak, ensuring our release
from the bleakness that has seized
thought, taking us from turbulence
that once assailed St Bridget with its buck and
    sway
and guiding shaken vessels back to peace.

---

*One of the Gaelic names for the oystercatcher is St Bridget's servant,
or* gille-Bràde. *This story is told about how it gained that name.*

One Good Reason to Remain in Lockdown

Inspired by Colum McCann's Apeirogon

It is safer to stay still.

Migrating birds are often killed
by everyday obstacles.

Such as steel pylons, the chill
of unexpected snowfall.
High windows.
Crops that either rot or fail.
Sandstorms. Occasional oil-spills.
Poison. Overflowing drains.
A jagged, rusty nail.

All reasons why it's wiser to remain
like the blackbird, starling, sparrow,
birds that rise and dip,
gorge and peck their fill
among the trees that grow
just beyond the space where I write,

outside the window-sill.

Shetland, June

The coming and going of boats punctuated her day. She would see them shifting back and forth between the window of her home and the lighthouse on the island of Bressay a short distance away. A fishing boat in a gleam of early morning light. A small ferry boat sailing in the direction of Lerwick in the early afternoon. An oil tanker arriving later in the day, taking up a long period of residence near one of the island's headlands, waiting for weeks there till prices rose at the petrol pump. And, of course, the main ferry sailing between five and six each evening, taking passengers with their masks and muffled voices south to Aberdeen, exchanging the tight boundaries of the islands for the twists and turns of narrow roads and motorways, the greater perils of the mainland at this time.

She misses the sounds these vessels used to make. When she was young, there would have been the phut-phut-phut of engines, the occasional jangle of a bell when those on one fishing boat approached another, a small gesture towards those who shared both their occupation and this thin stretch of water. Her sense of loss at this was at its most intense during these days when mist dulled the light of midsummer, fog draped these shores. At these moments, the view from her window was marked only by absence. No boats could be viewed passing through that narrow channel. No ferry could be seen steaming south. She reflected that it had not always been like that. Once there would have been blasts resonating through the haar when two vessels passed each other, these deep bass sounds marking both their progress and the hour of the day. There would have been hoots of welcome, warning notes, a medley of mechanical and other noises accompanying the cries and calls of gulls and other birds. She could even conjure up the ringing of a bell, the one her father rung when his trawler, the *Girl Margaret*, was returning from fishing in, perhaps, the North Sea or Pentland Firth, heading to the harbour with its hold full of fish.

Alone in her home, she often felt lonely and desolate without this accompaniment, one that would have been familiar to previous generations who occupied her home on the shoreline. She tried mimicking their noises, imitating the deep bass tones of a foghorn, the shrill sound of a whistle, the hoot of a fishing boat, even the thrum of an engine.

She was in the middle of impersonating these sounds when the postman came to her home, clutching an envelope with her name and an indecipherable address in his hand.

*

With each day of lockdown, her memory grew more uncertain. In the beginning, she behaved much the same as she had done before the whole phenomenon started, writing short reminders to herself about the items of grocery she had to purchase in the pages of a notebook she kept in a kitchen drawer. She did this religiously a few evenings a week, going out to purchase these household goods early on Saturday morning. It was a routine that began to falter when the hours and days of the week began to blur and become uniform. Saturday morning became confused with Wednesday evening; Sunday night edged into Tuesday afternoon. She wrote post-it notes to remind her of the exact date, sticking them on the correct date on the calendar, confusing herself later by forgetting to remove them when that day had passed.

As the persistent light of midsummer continued, all these actions occurred more frequently, becoming, too, more exact and precise. She started to write notes to herself about whether a particular hour was night or day, if she was brushing her teeth to go to bed or if she was doing this shortly after she had risen in the morning, if it was the time to take in or out the household bins. Knowing the local postman arrived most days relatively early, she would note his coming, scribbling the hour on the clock a few minutes after he had placed a letter in her hand. The problem with this arose on both Sunday and these rare days in the week when he failed to deliver the mail either in the morning or – indeed – at all. She became confused and anxious when these moments occurred, racing around to perform further tasks to prevent her losing the vestiges of her memory, writing down the names of the Queen, Prime Minister and First Minister of Scotland, fearing that some nurse or doctor might ask her who they were and she might somehow forget. She drew flags on post-it notes to remind her of the names of various countries. She sketched the outline of her birds that swirled around the house, the gulls and gannets that plunged into the bay on which her house overlooked, even the white tail and upright ears of a rabbit she had seen racing across the shoreline, scribbling the names of these creatures alongside to remind her exactly what they were.

Soon her fear of her failing memory began to dominate her life. Yellow post-it notes – some placed to remind her where previous notes had been stored – obliterated the wallpaper of her sitting room. They were fixed, too, on kitchen walls. They covered her bedroom, bathroom, the corridor of her home.

She was sticking one on the outside door when the postman arrived one day.

'Is this yours?' he asked.

She looked at it without saying anything, unsure whether it was or not.

'It's just that I can't make out the address. Someone looks as if they've forgotten what it is halfway through writing it out.'

She stared at it again, experiencing a faint sense that this might be her own handwriting. She wasn't entirely sure.

Quarff: 3 October

Our summer settlers have all vacated
their part-time residences on these shores. The
   terns long disappeared.
The occasional swallow and greylag geese
   migrated
to southern parts, no longer winging near
our northern homes. Sometimes I seek to
   visualise
the uproar that ensues when the cuckoo and the
   wheatear's flight
veers near the Mediterranean, or oystercatchers
   and hoopoes meet in skies
echoing with high calls and honking, when
   night's
no longer hushed and quiet in far-off towns,
when our former visitors throng telegraph poles
   or crumbling towers
in Italy or Africa, resting for a moment before
   spinning round
on journeys persevering for hour on endless
   hour.

Yet here the only sounds consist of a mixture of
   persistent wind,
the continual chirp and cheep
of starlings, the ticking of the clock we hear
   while being locked within

doors, the bleating of some nearby sheep.

That feeling still within us. The unseen presence
we can never comprehend.
The question we keep asking. When will all this
come to an end?

The Author

Originally from Ness, Isle of Lewis, former teacher Donald S Murray has lived for many years in Shetland. He is the author of numerous books, spanning non-fiction, fiction and poetry. Several have been selected as Guardian Nature Books of the Year. A Gaelic speaker, he also appears regularly on BBC Radio nan Gàidheal.

As the Women Lay Dreaming (Saraband), his first novel, was inspired by the effects of the tragic *Iolaire* disaster of 1st January 1919 on his home community in Lewis. The critically acclaimed novel was the subject of a documentary on BBC Alba and featured on BBC Radio 4's *Open Book*. As well as winning the Paul Torday Memorial Award, it was shortlisted for the Authors' Club First Novel Award, the Herald Award for an Outstanding Contribution to Scottish Culture, and was Highly Commended in the Sir Walter Scott Prize for Historical Fiction. His next novel, *In a Veil of Mist*, is forthcoming from Saraband in 2021. It returns to the Isle of Lewis and again considers the human cost of warfare and the perilous risks our nations take in waging war. A new non-fiction work, *For The Safety of All: the Story of Scotland's Lighthouses* (Historic Environment Scotland) will also appear in 2021.